THE TYPISTS AND THE TIGER

Murray Schisgal

THE TYPISTS AND THE TIGER

TWO PLAYS

INTRODUCED BY THE AUTHOR

Coward-McCann, Inc.
New York

Copyright © 1963 by Murray Schisgal

All rights reserved. This book, or parts thereof, may not be reproduced in any form without permission in writing from the Publisher. Published on the same day in the Dominion of Canada by Longmans Canada Limited, Toronto.

NOTICE. This play is the sole property of the author and is fully protected by copyright. It may not be acted by professionals or by amateurs without written consent. Public readings and radio or television broadcasts are likewise forbidden. All inquiries concerning rights should be addressed to the author's agent, Janet Roberts, Ashley-Steiner—Famous Artists, Inc., 555 Madison Avenue, New York 22, N. Y.

Photographs by courtesy of Arnold Newman

MANUFACTURED IN THE UNITED STATES OF AMERICA

To Reene

THE TYPISTS and THE TIGER opened in New York, February 4, 1963, at the Orpheum Theatre with Eli Wallach and Anne Jackson. The plays were presented by Claire Nichtern, directed by Arthur Storch, and the settings were designed by Wolfgang Roth.

Contents

PREFACE
11

THE TYPISTS
15

THE TIGER
75

PREFACE

Passing through London on the way to Spain a few summers ago, I gave, without much optimism, three short plays I had written (*The Typists* and *The Tiger* were among them) to a small theatrical group that worked at the British Drama League. Almost at once I was told that they would be produced. This came as quite a surprise. Until then I had never seriously thought of the European theatre as being essential, psychologically as well as practically, to the American playwright.

The plays were done and I came back to New York, without ever having reached Spain. Within two weeks I was called back to London. *The Typists* was taped for British television, productions at the Edinburgh Festival and in Israel were arranged. While in London this second time, Michael Codron and David Hall, producers, took an option on a long play of mine. I returned to New York, finished another play, *Ducks and Lovers*, and sent it off to them. They decided to do this play instead of the other, and once again I returned to London. *Ducks and Lovers* was produced at the Arts Theatre in December, 1961. I returned home. A month later I was back in London, writing the scenario of *Ducks and Lovers* for an English movie company. And while in London this fourth time, Oscar Lewenstein took an option on my latest play, *Luv*.

My experience is not, I'm sure, so very unique. What is

PREFACE

unique is the knowledge that American playwrights are beginning to share: the knowledge that the European theatre is more valuable to him in certain instances than the theatre at home. This is particularly true if he is a newcomer or if his play brings forth the shibboleth of "commercial feasibility." I find none of this dismaying. A bit peculiar, perhaps.

MURRAY SCHISGAL

The Typists

THE TIME:
At twenty-odd years of age.

THE SCENE:
An office: forward, center, a pair of simple metal typewriter tables, with leaves extended, on which there are two old standard typewriters, stacks of postcards, and a bulky telephone directory on each; rear, a large window, two tall green steel file cabinets, a desk between them on which there are a great many telephone directories and a telephone, a door to the restroom; at the right wall, forward, a water cooler, a wooden coat hanger, the entrance door; in the left wall, the door to the employer's office.

The sun streams through the window; as the play progresses it fades imperceptibly until, at the end, the room is almost in complete darkness.

The same clothes are worn throughout by the actors, although altered to suit the physical changes—subtle, almost unnoticed when they occur—that take place during the course of the play.

The Typists

SYLVIA PAYTON *enters from right. She is late for work. She throws her coat on the hanger, rushes across the room, deposits her lunch bag in the top drawer of a cabinet, removes cover from her typewriter and begins typing rapidly, glancing anxiously at the employer's door. In a moment she relaxes; she types slowly and hums to herself; she takes her comb and mirror from her pocketbook and fixes her hair. The front door opens. She puts everything away and without turning to see who has entered she starts to type rapidly again.* PAUL CUNNINGHAM *approaches, passing his lunch bag from hand to hand.*

PAUL

Good morning. I'm Paul Cunningham. I was hired yesterday by . . .
    (*Laughing uneasily*)
That's funny. I forgot his name. You'll have to excuse me. First day on the job . . . I'm a little nervous. It was the boss who hired me, though; at least that's what he said.

SYLVIA

I know. He told me.
    (*Rising, shaking his hand*)
Sylvia. Miss Sylvia Payton. Glad to meet you, Mr. Cunningham. If you'll hang up your coat I'll show you what you have to do.

PAUL

I'm sorry I'm late, Miss Payton. I got on the wrong train by mistake. Generally you'll find that I'm a pretty prompt person.

SYLVIA

Oh, that's all right. Just make sure it doesn't happen too often. He's very strict when it comes to being here on time. And now that he's made me responsible for this whole department . . . Of course I won't say anything to him about this morning.

PAUL

I'd appreciate that a lot.

SYLVIA

Don't even mention it. Believe me, I didn't ask him to be made a supervisor. I don't like telling anyone what to do; that's part of my nature, I guess. You give me your lunch bag, Mr. Cunningham. I'll put it in the file cabinet; that's where I keep mine.

PAUL

Thanks. I was sure lucky to get this job. I go to school at night and a lot of firms don't hire you if they know that.

SYLVIA

You must be a very ambitious person. What are you studying?

PAUL

(*Proudly*)
Law. Another three years and I should get my degree. Boy, that's one day I'm looking forward to.

The Typists

SYLVIA

It must be extremely difficult to have a job and go to school at the same time.

PAUL

It's been real rough so far. But it has its advantages. When I get out, I'm going to have the satisfaction of knowing I did it myself, with my own sweat and my own money; that's more than most fellows my age can say.

SYLVIA

How true that is.

PAUL

Listen, I have an uncle who's a lawyer, a pretty darn famous lawyer, too. Francis T. Cunningham. You ask anybody in the legal field about Francis T. Cunningham and they'll tell you how much he's worth. Well, if I wanted to, I just have to pick up that phone, give him a ring and my worrying days would be over. But that's not for me; no, sir. I'll do it alone or I'm not doing it at all.

SYLVIA

(*Uncovers* PAUL's *typewriter, opens directory for him*)
I think you're a hundred percent right. You know, I once went with a boy—it was nothing serious, it could have been, but . . . I won't go into that now. Anyway, his father was helping him through medical school. He didn't have to earn a penny of his own. Do you think he finished? What happened was that his father remarried and stopped

[18

giving him money. He fell completely apart; you never saw anything like it.

PAUL
There's no substitute for character.

SYLVIA
That's exactly the point. Well, we'd better get to work before he starts screaming. We're on a promotion campaign now and it's a very important job. I suppose that's why you were hired. What we do is type out the names and addresses of prospective customers on these postcards. The advertisement is printed on the back. We get the information we want straight from the telephone book. Don't leave out any names; go right down the line. He checks everything and he can be awfully mean if he wants to. I've just started on the A's, so you'll start with the . . .

PAUL
B's.

SYLVIA
Right. That way we'll be sure to get everyone.

PAUL
It sounds easy enough.

SYLVIA
It is. And after awhile you can do it without even thinking.
 (*They are both seated, typing*)

THE TYPISTS

PAUL

Ooops! My first card and my first mistake. I'm afraid I'm a little rusty. I haven't been doing much typing lately.
(*He is about to throw card into basket*)

SYLVIA

No, don't throw it away. If he sees it, he'll raise the roof. At the beginning you ought to type more slowly. Lean back in your chair. Posture's very important. And strike each key with the same steady rhythm.

PAUL

Like this?

SYLVIA

Better, much better; don't move your head; keep your eyes on the material you're typing.

PAUL

(*Sitting rigidly, uncomfortably*)
It's really nice of you to help me this way.

SYLVIA

I'm only too glad to, Mr. Cunningham.

PAUL

Paul.

SYLVIA

(*Staring at him, warmly*)
Paul.

The Typists

(*The buzzer rings once*)
That's for me.
(*Quickly tidying herself*)
He doesn't usually call me in this early. You go on with your work, Paul. He gets furious when he doesn't hear these typewriters going. He probably wants to know why it took us so long to get started this morning. Don't worry. I'll cover up for you.

PAUL

(*Holding her arm*)
Thanks for everything, Sylvia.

SYLVIA

You're welcome . . . Paul.
(*Paul watches her as she swings her hips self-consciously and exits to employer's office. He then starts to type, makes an error, crumples card and is about to throw it into basket; on second thought he slips the card into his pocket. Again he types and makes an error, looks guiltily toward the employer's office and slips card into his pocket. All the while he whistles to the tune of "Way Down Upon The Swanee River . . ."*)

SYLVIA

(*Entering, angrily*)
He's got some goddamn nerve! What does he think I am, a child? I see it doesn't pay to be nice to people. Well, he can just go and look for someone else to do his dirty work. I'm leaving!
(*Gathers her things together*)

The Typists

PAUL
What happened?

SYLVIA
Bawling me out for being five minutes late; that's nerve, believe me.

PAUL
(*Laughing*)
So you were late this morning, too?

SYLVIA
There's nothing funny about it, Paul. When you've devoted as much time and energy as I have to this firm, giving them the best you're capable of, then maybe you'll see things differently. Where are my gloves?

PAUL
(*Rising, gives them to her*)
Here they are. Listen, Sylvia; you're excited. Why don't you think about it, huh?

SYLVIA
There's nothing to think about. When he asks you where I went, you just tell him for me that I don't care to associate with a firm that has no feelings for its employees.
(*She struggles with coat; he helps her put it on*)

PAUL
It's not easy finding a job now, I can tell you that.

SYLVIA
With my experience? You must be joking. I've been made many many offers in the past that I've refused out of a sense of loyalty to that . . . to that sex maniac in there. This is my reward.

PAUL
I wouldn't give him the satisfaction; no, sir.

SYLVIA
What satisfaction?

PAUL
Well, it stands to reason that he wanted you to quit, doesn't it? He knows you're a sensitive girl. By leaving you're doing just what he wants.

SYLVIA
You think he deliberately . . .

PAUL
Why else would he have bawled you out?

SYLVIA
(Slight pause; takes off coat, puts it on hanger)
I'd die before I gave him the satisfaction. If that's what he has in mind, he's got another guess coming. I'm leaving at my convenience, not his.

PAUL
Now you're talking.

The Typists

SYLVIA

Believe me, there'll come a day when he'll really need me. "Miss Payton, won't you please help me get this job through in time?" Then it'll be my turn. I'll just laugh right in his stupid face and walk out.

PAUL

Boy, I'd like to be here to see it. Is he married?

SYLVIA

Who would marry him? Ugly as sin, that's what he is.
(*They type, laugh over the noise of their typing, then suddenly stop*)

SYLVIA

We had a girl working here once; she was a riot. She used to draw these caricatures and mail them to him; anonymously, of course. But you should have seen them; they were the funniest thing.
(*They type, laugh, stop suddenly*)

PAUL

The last job I had was for this woman, Mrs. Jameson. She was as blind as a bat without her glasses. You know what we used to do? Whenever we got the chance we hid her glasses somewhere in the office. For two or three days until she'd find them, we didn't have to do anything, not a single piece of work. We just sat around talking all day.

SYLVIA

I was with an insurance company when I graduated from

high school. There was this man in charge there, Mr. Williams, his name was, and he used to have loose hands, if you know what I mean.

PAUL

I know.

SYLVIA

Well, one day he was telling me how to type a policy and he let his hands fall—very, very casually—on my shoulder. So I turned around and looked up at him and spat right in his face.

PAUL

You were fired, I bet.

SYLVIA

As a matter of fact we got along very well after that.
   (*They type; stop suddenly; turn to one another*)

PAUL

Have you read any good books lately?

SYLVIA

I read a very good detective novel last week. It was called *Murder in Bombay*.

PAUL

I'm a science fiction man myself.
   (*They type; stop suddenly; turn to one another*)

THE TYPISTS

SYLVIA

Can I ask you something?

PAUL

Sure. What is it?

SYLVIA

If you had to choose between getting a million dollars or losing a leg which would you take?

PAUL

Right leg or left leg?

SYLVIA

Any leg.

PAUL

(*Pause*)
I'd take the million dollars.

SYLVIA

I wouldn't. I'd keep my legs.
    (*They type; stop suddenly. They both stare at the audience,* PAUL *leaning forward,* SYLVIA *back in her chair, her face expressionless, her hands in her lap*)

PAUL

I was born in a poor section of Brooklyn. My parents were at each other's throat most of the time. It was a miserable childhood. I had no brothers or sisters; there was only the three of us living in this old run-down house, with cats cry-ing and screaming all night in the alley. Why my parents ever got married, I don't know, and why they stayed together for as long as they did I don't know that either. They're separated now. But it doesn't much matter anymore. They were as unlike as any two people could be. All my father wanted was to be left alone to smoke his pipe and listen to the radio. My mother—she was a pretty woman, she knew how to dress, all right—she liked to go out and enjoy herself. I was stuck between the two of them and they pulled on both sides. I couldn't talk to one without the other accusing me of being ungrateful; I couldn't touch or kiss one of them without being afraid that the other one would see me and there would be a fight. I had to keep my thoughts to myself. I had to grow up wishing for some kind of miracle. I remember coming home from school one afternoon. I must have been twelve or thirteen. There was this man in the living room with my mother. They weren't doing anything; they were just sitting and talking. But I felt that something was going on. I seemed to stop breathing and I ran out of the house and threw up on the curbstone. Later on I swore to myself that I would make a miracle happen; that I wouldn't ever have to be where I didn't want to be and I wouldn't have to do what I didn't want to do; that I could be myself, without being afraid. But it's rough. With a background like mine you're always trying to catch up; it's as if you were born two steps behind the next fellow.

(*They type; stop suddenly. They both stare at the audience,* SYLVIA *leaning forward,* PAUL *back in his chair, etc.*)

The Typists

SYLVIA

My family never had money problems. In that respect we were very fortunate. My father made a good living, while he was alive, that is. He passed away when I was seventeen. You could say he and my mother had a fairly happy marriage. At least we never knew when they were angry with one another, and that's a good thing for children. I have a sister. Charlotte. She's older than I am. She's married now and we don't bother much with each other. But when we were younger you wouldn't believe what went on. Every time we quarreled, according to my parents she was right; I was always wrong. She got everything she wanted, no matter what, and I had to be content with the leftovers. It was just unbearable. Anyway, my father was sick for a long time before he passed away. He had this ring, it was a beautiful ring, with a large onyx stone in it, and when I was a girl I used to play with it. I'd close one eye and I'd look inside of it and I'd see hundreds and hundreds of beautiful red and blue stars. My father had always promised me that ring; he always said it belonged to me. I thought for certain he'd give it to me before he passed away, but he didn't say anything about it; not a word. Well, afterward, I saw it. You know where I saw it? On my sister's finger. He had given it to her. Now I don't think that's a background that leaves many possibilities for development. I don't forgive my father; definitely not. And I don't forgive my sister. My mother, whom I now support with my hard work, still says I'm wrong.

(*They type; stop suddenly; turn to one another*)

PAUL

Do you go to the movies?

SYLVIA

Not too often.

PAUL

Me neither.

SYLVIA

Do you like to watch television?

PAUL

I never get the chance. Don't forget I go to school five nights a week. But my wife watches it a lot; that's all she does.

SYLVIA

(*Surprised*)
I didn't know you were married.

PAUL

(*Types*)
This machine's full of errors. I'm getting nowhere fast.
    (*He is about to crumple card*)

SYLVIA

(*Rising*)
Let me see that, please.
    (*Examines card, incommensurate anger*)
Now this could be erased. We don't approve of wasting

The Typists

material when it can be saved. That isn't the policy of this office.

PAUL

Okay. You don't have to be mad. I'll do it.

SYLVIA

I'm not mad. But I am responsible for what goes on in this department. I'm sick and tired of covering up for your mistakes. Everyone must think I'm a piece of rag to be stepped on. First him and now you.

PAUL

Do you mind telling me what you're talking about!

SYLVIA

You know very well what I'm talking about. This is my thanks; this is what I get for trying to be helpful and nice to people. I'm wrong, I know. I'm always wrong. Everything I do is wrong. Well, Mr. Cunningham, I've had enough, quite enough, and I won't take any more from you or anyone else. I won't! I won't!

(*She flees to the restroom. Paul slaps the typewriter, goes to telephone, dials*)

PAUL

(*Loudly*)

Let me speak to Mr. Francis T. Cunningham, please. Who's calling? Paul Cunningham!

(*Softly*)

Hello, Uncle Frank. It's me again. Paul. How . . . how are you? Everything all right? That's good. Oh, everything's

fine with me; still plugging away. I got a new job; yeah, typing, office work; just enough for bread. Uhuh. Uncle, can't you give me a hand? It's too rough for me. I can't hold down a job and go to school five nights a week; it's killing me. I know, I know. But I thought if you could give me a part-time job in your office, or maybe one of your friends, if you spoke to them . . . Yeah, sure. I understand. It's okay. Yeah. Send my regards.
> (PAUL *returns to typewriter.* SYLVIA *enters, exchanges her directory. Her appearance is that of a woman in her thirties*)

SYLVIA

I'm sorry for losing my temper, Paul. It won't happen again.

PAUL

Forget it.
> (*He types*)

SYLVIA

You've become an expert at that machine.

PAUL

> (*Glumly*)

At least I'm an expert at something.

SYLVIA

Is anything the matter?

PAUL

No, but I was just thinking. What am I knocking myself

out for? School almost every night, weekends I'm home studying, I can't remember the last time I took a decent vacation. What for? You're young only once; this is the time to enjoy yourself.

SYLVIA

(*At typewriter*)
I don't know how true that is. You probably could enjoy yourself a great deal more if you were a lawyer; that's why some sacrifices have to be made now.

PAUL

That's the kind of logic that leads nowhere. By your reasoning all lawyers should be happy men. No, sir; that isn't the way life is. You could be a ditch-digger and be happy if you know how to live. I tell you, I've had it. A fellow in my position has to take advantage of what's offered to him. He's got to be practical and look the facts right in the eye.
(*Tapping table*)
This here is what's offered to me. This is my chance and from now on I start concentrating on this job. I'll show him I'm on the ball and maybe he'll find something else for me, give me a promotion, a better salary. Why not? An outfit this big always needs men who aren't afraid to work. Listen, I've got two kids at home. I've got to start thinking of them, too.

SYLVIA

(*Stiffly*)
You have two children?

PAUL

Sure. I don't waste any time. Look, I've got their pictures here. We took these last summer.
    (*He shows her photographs inside wallet*)
Well, what do you think?

SYLVIA

    (*Coldly*)
They're beautiful, Paul. What's their names?

PAUL

Frank and Sally. But we call the boy Buddy; he hates it when we call him Frank; funny rascal. They're not bad for a character like me, are they? You know what I'm going to do, Syl? I'm going right in to him and ask him what my chances for advancement are. I might as well get all this settled now. Frankly I can use a little more money, too. The expenses are killing me. If we had a union in this place, we'd get some action. I may do something about that yet.
    (*He heads for employer's office, turns*)
What . . . what would you say is the best way to approach him?

SYLVIA

I honestly don't know, Paul. He changes from one minute to the next. But if he isn't wearing his glasses, that's a bad sign; I know that much.

PAUL

Glasses . . . I got it. Wish me luck?

THE TYPISTS

SYLVIA

I hope you get something good.
(*After* PAUL *exits, she goes to phone, dials*)
Ma? Sylvia. No, I'm all right. Did the lamp come? Well, just make sure when it comes that it isn't damaged; you'll have to sign for it and that means you inspected it. Look at it carefully; if there isn't any damage you can sign, but if there's anything wrong with it, the smallest thing, refuse to sign and tell the man to take it back. Do you understand? I hope so. Did I . . . get any calls? I didn't say I was expecting any, don't put words in my mouth, I merely asked you if I got any. Never mind. It's not important. Did Charlotte call? How is she?
(PAUL *enters. He has the appearance of a man in his thirties.* SYLVIA *carries on the remainder of her call as though talking to a boyfriend*)

SYLVIA

Oh, stop being silly. I really couldn't. I have something this Saturday. I mean it.
(*Laughing*)
No, no. Well, perhaps Sunday. Call me at home. All right. Bye.

PAUL

(*At typewriter*)
It looks good, real good. He's considering it. He says they may need someone on the sales staff. I'm first on the list.

SYLVIA

That does sound good. What about the raise?

[34

PAUL
I'll have to wait awhile, he said. But I'll get it. He was impressed, especially when I told him I had some legal experience. You should have seen his eyes open up. It's only a question of time, and once I start moving, you watch, it's going to take a pretty fast man to keep up with me.

SYLVIA
You certainly have ambition, Paul.

PAUL
(*Rises to exchange directory*)
Listen, I don't intend to spend the rest of my life working here or any place else. I'll make my bundle and that's it. There's a world outside that window, a world with a thousand different things to see and do, and I'm going to see and do every last one of them; you watch.

SYLVIA
There's a million different things to do in the world.

PAUL
Lie in the sun . . .

SYLVIA
Dance . . .

PAUL
Travel . . .

SYLVIA
Wear pretty clothes . . .

THE TYPISTS

              PAUL
Visit places . . .

              SYLVIA
Meet interesting people . . .

              PAUL
Mountains. A place with mountains . . .

              SYLVIA
(*Grabs* PAUL's *lapels, her emotions soaring*)
Oh, Paul, I'm so filled with the desire to live, to experience things, to laugh . . . Oh, I want to laugh, Paul!
    (*Silence.* PAUL *stares dumbly at her, clears his throat. Stiffly they return to their chairs, type energetically*)

              PAUL
(*In a moment, calmly*)
When do we have lunch?

              SYLVIA
We can have it any time we want. But I usually have it at one. The later you have it the shorter the afternoon is.

              PAUL
How about waiting until one-thirty?

              SYLVIA
That isn't easy.

PAUL
I know, but then we'd only have a couple of more hours to go. The afternoon would fly. What do you say?

SYLVIA
I'm willing, if you are.

PAUL
It's a deal, then. One-thirty lunch.
  (*They shake hands*)

SYLVIA
One-thirty.

PAUL
Right.
  (*They both type*)

SYLVIA
You know, I'm getting hungry already.

PAUL
So am I. I didn't have any breakfast.

SYLVIA
I had a cup of coffee, that's all.

PAUL
What have you got for lunch?

The Typists

SYLVIA
A tuna-fish sandwich with tomatoes and mayonnaise, an orange and a piece of layer cake. What did you bring?

PAUL
Two turkey sandwiches and an apple, I think.

SYLVIA
One-thirty.
   (*They shake hands*)

PAUL
That's the deal.
   (*They both type*)

PAUL
We went down to Chinatown last weekend. What a meal we had.

SYLVIA
I'm crazy about Chinese food. I once went with a fellow who knew how to speak Chinese and you should have seen the things he ordered; the most fantastic dishes, with chicken livers and mushrooms and almonds . . .

PAUL
The Chinese people can cook, all right, but when it comes to *real* cooking you can't beat the Italians. There's a place we go to on the West Side; you should taste their veal parmesan or their chicken cacciatore. And they make a spaghetti sauce, you could . . .

SYLVIA

(*Goes to file cabinet*)
I think I'll eat now.

PAUL

(*Rising, furiously*)
We made a deal, didn't we?

SYLVIA

Don't be childish. If I want to eat now, I'll eat now, and that's all there is to it.

PAUL

You women are all alike. No backbone. No self-discipline. Go ahead and eat, I'm not going to stop you. But I'm sticking to my word.

SYLVIA

I didn't say I was going to eat, Mr. Cunningham. I merely said I was thinking of eating; listen before you speak.
(*She waves at him blank postcards which she has taken from cabinet*)
And if you want to know something else, I could probably wait longer than you; I could probably go without lunch, which is more than some people can say.

PAUL

(*At typewriter*)
Is that so?

SYLVIA

(At *typewriter*)
That's so exactly.

PAUL

We'll see, Miss Supervisor.

SYLVIA

You're jealous. It's coming out all over you. I am supervisor . . .

PAUL

(*Waving his arm*)
Of this whole department. Boy, I'll never forget that as long as I live.
(*Mimicking her in a small voice*)
"Believe me, Mr. Cunningham, I didn't ask him to be made supervisor. I don't like telling anyone what to do; that's part of my nature . . ."
(*He falls on typewriter in a fit of laughter*)

SYLVIA

You just keep that up and you won't be working here much longer, I assure you of that, Mr. Cunningham.

PAUL

Tell him. Go ahead and tell him. You'd be doing me a favor!

SYLVIA

What? You mean a man with your legal experience, with your plans and ambitions, requires a favor from me?

PAUL
Miss Payton, I loathe you!

SYLVIA
That, Mr. Cunningham, would be a gross understatement to describe my feelings for you. You make me sick!

PAUL
Why don't you quit, then?

SYLVIA
Why don't you?

PAUL
I wouldn't give you the satisfaction.

SYLVIA
And I wouldn't give you the satisfaction!
(*They both type, loudly, rapidly*)

PAUL
(*Slaps keys*)
What the hell am I doing? This isn't what I want. No, goddamn it!

SYLVIA
(*Without looking at him*)
I wonder if the man knows what he wants.

THE TYPISTS

PAUL

(*Almost ominously*)
You bet I do. And do you know what it is? You know what I'd really like to do? Now, right here in this office?
(*Rises, moves around* SYLVIA's *chair*)
I'd like to rip the clothes right off your back, piece by piece. I'd like to dig my fingers into your flesh and feel your body break and sweat under mine. Do you understand me, Miss Payton?

SYLVIA

(*Rises; softly*)
Paul.

PAUL

It's been eating me up, ever since I first saw you. I want you, Miss Payton. Now! Now! This minute! Here, on the floor, screaming your lungs out and with your legs kicking up in the air. That's all I've been thinking of at that stupid typewriter; that's all that's been on my mind.
(*Pause*)
Now you know.

SYLVIA

And what do you think I've been thinking of? My body aches with wanting you, Paul.
(*Turning, pointing to his typewriter*)
How many times have I closed my eyes, just hoping you'd do something instead of sitting there like a stone statue!
(*She falls back into him; he embraces her around the waist, standing behind her*)

[42

PAUL

Sylvia.

SYLVIA

I'll have to tell my mother, Paul. And you should tell your wife. Oh, I'll be good to the children. I promise you that.

PAUL

(*Stunned*)
Tell my wife?

SYLVIA

We will get married, won't we?

PAUL

Sylvia, listen . . .

SYLVIA

(*Turning to face him*)
We will get married, won't we?

PAUL

Aw, the hell with it! I'm going to eat.
(*Gets lunch bag, throws coat over arm*)

SYLVIA

(*At typewriter*)
It's my fault, I know; you don't have to tell me.

PAUL

It's nobody's fault. It's . . . the way things are.
(*At door*)
Can I get you anything?

THE TYPISTS

SYLVIA

I'm not eating.

PAUL

Suit yourself.
(PAUL *exits.* SYLVIA *runs to cabinet, takes out lunch bag; she eats her sandwich ravenously. The door is suddenly thrown open. Quickly* SYLVIA *turns, clutching the sandwich to her chest, hiding it*)

PAUL

Are you sure you don't want anything?

SYLVIA

(*With a mouthful of food*)
Positive.

PAUL

All right.
(PAUL *exits.* SYLVIA *goes to the phone, slowly, lethargically, dials*)

SYLVIA

Ma? Sylvia. Nothing's wrong. I'm having my lunch now. The sandwich is fine. Did the table come? How is it? Are you sure? Sometimes they get damaged in shipping. Did you look carefully? Well, I hope so. Yes. Did I get any calls? No, I wasn't expecting any; I just asked.
(*Pause*)

What did Charlotte say? That's just like her. She could come at least once a week to see how you are. All right, have it your own way. I'm too tired to argue with you. How are the children? That's nice.

(*Pause*)

An eighty-five average doesn't mean he's a genius; no, not by any stretch of the imagination. I'm not saying she has stupid children; that isn't what I said, but I can't stand it when you raise them to the sky. I repeat, an eighty-five average is not in the genius class, and if you want proof ask anyone in the educational field. Oh, all right, all right; let's just drop it. I'll see you later. Of course I'm coming home. Where do you think I'd go? Fine. Good-bye.

>(SYLVIA *throws the remainder of her sandwich into basket, reluctantly sits down at typewriter. As she types and swings the carriage across—for want of something to do—she sings the material she is typing with the lilting intonation of a small girl bouncing a ball on the sidewalk while reciting doggerel*)

SYLVIA

(*Typing*)

Mrs. Anna Robinson, of 4 East 32nd Street, in the city and state of New York.

>(*Taking card out, putting new card in; forlornly*)

How are you today, Mrs. Anna Robinson? It has been so nice talking to you. Who have we here? Oh, it's

(*Typing*)

Mr. Arnold Robinson, of 1032 Lexington Avenue, in the city and state of New York.

>(*Taking card out, putting new card in*)

THE TYPISTS

It was so pleasant talking to you, Mr. Robinson. Send my regards to the family. Why, if it isn't
    (*Typing*)
Mrs. Beatrice Robinson, who lives no less on Park Avenue, in the city and state of New York.
    (*Taking card out, putting new card in*)
Must you leave so soon, Mrs. Robinson?
    (SYLVIA *takes a gumdrop from a bag of candy, continues typing.* PAUL *enters. He is now in his forties. He carries a container of coffee*)

PAUL
(*Referring to her candy*)
Up to your old tricks again, Sylvia? You'll never keep your figure that way.

SYLVIA
Don't worry about my figure; just worry about your own.

PAUL
(*Pulling his stomach in*)
You've got a point there. Here, I brought you some coffee.

SYLVIA
Thanks.
    (*Gets newspaper*)
How is it outside?

PAUL
A little chilly, but the sun's strong; nice. I took a walk up to the park. You never saw so many characters sitting on

[46

the benches and sunning themselves. I sure would like to know how they do it.

SYLVIA
Half of them are probably on relief.

PAUL
We work and they sun themselves.

SYLVIA
You should see the cars some of them have.

PAUL
You don't have to tell me. I know.

SYLVIA
I read in the newspapers that by the year 2000 people will work only three hours a day and have a three-day week.

PAUL
That's not going to help me.

SYLVIA
(At *typewriter; opens newspaper*)
We could try to get into a union.

PAUL
Do you know one that isn't crooked?

SYLVIA
How I wish this day was over.

The Typists

PAUL
It'll feel good getting these shoes off.

SYLVIA
I'll wash my hair and do a little ironing.

PAUL
No date tonight?

SYLVIA
Don't be funny.

PAUL
(At typewriter)
You know, I was thinking, Syl. Ever since I was a kid I always thought I would like to be independent, to live my own life, without getting involved with responsibilities and families. Inside of me I suppose I always was afraid of that. But, you know, everything I've done in my life has taken me away from what I thought I'd like to be when I was a kid. I got married as soon as I could; I had children right away; I made it so tough for myself I couldn't get through law school. I couldn't live the kind of life I thought I wanted. I've been asking myself lately, what is it I really wanted? You know what the answer to that is, Syl? You know what it has to be? What I got. What I am. Maybe all I really wanted was to be sorry for myself.

SYLVIA
Does anyone know what they want, Paul?

PAUL
Don't you?

SYLVIA
Not any more. I thought I knew, just as you did. But if that's what I wanted, why am I where I am today?

PAUL
It doesn't make sense, does it?

SYLVIA
I swore that at the first opportunity I'd break away from my mother and my sister; I'd have nothing more to do with them and that would be happiness for me. But here I am still living with my mother and every day I ask how my sister is, what she's doing, how her husband is, the children . . . And I don't give a damn. Not a damn.

PAUL
The things I don't give a damn about . . . Syl, let's look into it. This is important.

SYLVIA
I've always said there's nothing more important than getting to know yourself. When you realize that people can live their whole lives without knowing themselves, without really getting to understand themselves, it . . . it reaches the ridiculous.

PAUL
(*Rising*)
You're absolutely right.

THE TYPISTS

SYLVIA
(*Rising*)
Let's see what's behind it all. Let's study it a moment.

PAUL
All right, let's get to it. Why?

SYLVIA
Why?

PAUL
Why do you say that leaving your family would make you happy? If that's all there was to it, you could have left them years ago. No, there's something you're hiding.

SYLVIA
You're not telling the truth. If all you wanted was to feel sorry for yourself, all you'd have to do is sit in a corner and feel sorry for yourself; that's all there is to it. But, no; that isn't it.

PAUL
Then what is it?

SYLVIA
What are you hiding?
> (*As one speaks, wagging a finger, the other paces back and forth, nodding without listening, following a separate train of thought*)

PAUL

The fact remains that you do care what happens to your family, you care a lot, an awful lot; that's why you phone every day, that's why you're always asking about your sister. You have to keep them together; you need them more than they need you because you never developed emotionally enough to forget the past and start a new life for yourself.

SYLVIA

You deliberately put yourself in situations in which you had to fail. Why is it I never heard you say you loved your wife? What was behind your marriage at such an early age? Why didn't you wait until you finished school so that you'd have a fair chance of getting ahead?

PAUL

Simply because you wanted something from them. It had nothing to do with your father's ring; you use that for a smoke screen.

SYLVIA

Now we're coming closer to the truth. You had to rush into marriage, have children and become burdened with impossible responsibilities, the very things you were afraid of; you had to fail because it wasn't that you wanted to feel sorry for yourself, but you wanted other people to feel sorry for you.

PAUL

That's it! They alone could give you what you wanted; no one else, not even a husband; that's why you never got married. Now we're coming closer to it . . .

THE TYPISTS

> SYLVIA

So that they would pity and pamper you like a child; you mistook that for love, which was what you really wanted from them, the love which you couldn't get from your parents.
> (*They suddenly stand face-to-face*)

> PAUL

There it is! You wanted love!

> SYLVIA

You wanted love, of course!

> PAUL

Don't you see it now, Syl?

> SYLVIA

It's all so clear.

> PAUL

When you know something about yourself, then you can start doing something about it.
> (*They march back to their typewriters*)

> SYLVIA

This has been one of the most pleasant conversations I've ever had, Paul.

> PAUL

I enjoyed it myself.
> (*Glancing at wristwatch*)

And the afternoon's going pretty fast.

SYLVIA

Thank God for that.
(*They both type*)

PAUL

You know, thinking about it. I'm sure a lot better off than you are.

SYLVIA

Why's that?

PAUL

Well, I've got a place of my own; I did marry, have children. You could say I fulfilled a pretty important part of my life.

SYLVIA

That's nonsense. Do you think it requires any special ability to get married and have children?

PAUL

All I'm saying is that there are some people who would be awfully glad if they could have gotten married.

SYLVIA

Are you referring to me, Mr. Cunningham?

PAUL

I didn't mention any names, did I? But if the shoe fits, wear it, Miss Payton!

SYLVIA

(*Grimly*)
Don't make me laugh. If I had to make the choice—and I assure you I don't—I would much prefer being single than being forced to continue an unhappy marriage.

PAUL

An unhappy marriage? Where do you get that from? Did you ever hear me say that?

SYLVIA

I can put one and one together, Mr. Cunningham. We both know that if you had your way about it you would have left her long ago.

PAUL

Is that right?

SYLVIA

That's exactly right.

PAUL

Well, for your information, Miss Payton, my wife is the finest (*Rising*), do you hear me? The finest, the most decent woman I ever had the good fortune to meet.

SYLVIA

Please, Mr. Cunningham.

PAUL

And for your further information, I wouldn't trade her for a dozen like you.

SYLVIA
You couldn't possibly.
    (*The buzzer rings; she fixes her hair, etc.*)
Thank God, at last I'll have a moment away from you.

PAUL
I bet you think I don't know what goes on in there?

SYLVIA
What is he raving about now?

PAUL
Go ahead in. I can hear your boyfriend panting behind the door.

SYLVIA
Jealous?

PAUL
Of you?

SYLVIA
It's happened before.

PAUL
    (*Turning away from her, loud undertone*)
You bitch!

SYLVIA
    (*Turning, flaring*)
What did you say?
    (*No answer*)

The Typists

You'd better be quiet.

> (*She exits.* PAUL *goes to hanger and without unwrapping or removing the whiskey bottle from his coat pocket pours a drink into a water cup, swallows it, then fills the cup again. He dials the phone*)

PAUL

Barbara. Paul. How're the kids? That's good. Oh, pretty much the same. Listen, Barb, I'm . . . I'm sorry about last night. I had a little too much to drink. No, no, don't go excusing it. I just want you to know I didn't mean any of it. I think an awful . . . an awful lot of you, you know that, and I respect you, I always have. It's when I'm drinking, it's the whiskey that does the talking. I'm going to stop, I promise you. Barb, you forgive me, don't you? Well, say it; I want to hear you say it; please.

> (*Pause*)

Thank you. I'll try to get home early and we'll do something, we'll do something different, something . . . different, I promise you. All right. Don't forget. So long.

> (*He finishes his drink, crumples cup and slips it into his pocket. Sylvia enters, carrying several sheets of paper, which she places on Paul's typewriter. She is now in her forties*)

SYLVIA

He wants you to type copies of these. He's waiting for them.

PAUL

What's that?

SYLVIA

(*At typewriter*)
You heard me.

PAUL

Well, you hear me now. You can go right in there and tell him to go to hell. I'm not his secretary.

SYLVIA

Why don't you tell him yourself?

PAUL

That's a good idea!
    (*Moves to employer's office, grabbing papers from typewriter, turns*)
That's a damn good idea!
    (*Exits*)

SYLVIA

(*Typing, singsong, as before*)
Mr. Thomas Weaver, of 424 Harley Street, in the Bronx, New York.
    (*Taking card out, putting card in*)
I hope that you're having a pleasant day, Mr. Thomas Weaver. Now who is this coming along? Oh, it's
    (*Typing*)
Miss Tina Lee Weaver, of number 78 Monroe Avenue, in the Bronx, New York. How are you . . .
    (*Paul enters. He shouts at employer's door as he rips papers in half and throws them in the air*)

The Typists

           PAUL
There, there, that's what I think of you and your job, you old bastard!

           SYLVIA
Paul!

           PAUL
Why don't you go in and see your boyfriend now? You'll see him hiding behind the desk. If he stayed on his feet like a man I would have punched him right in the nose.

           SYLVIA
Did you . . . quit?

           PAUL
What the hell do you think I did? Trying to pull that stuff on me. I'm not his secretary and I never was.
    (*Shouting at employer's door*)
Do you hear me, you old bastard! I'm not your secretary and I never was!

           SYLVIA
    (*Rising, with concern*)
Please, Paul, be quiet; you're in enough trouble.

           PAUL
Trouble? Me? Ha! That's the funniest thing I heard yet. You're looking at a free man, Miss Payton; a free and independent man. Yes, sir. I haven't felt this good in years.

SYLVIA
(*Following him to coat hanger*)
But what will you do?

PAUL
(*Removing whiskey bottle from coat, throwing wrapper away*)
Start living for one thing; start being myself; start being a man again. You know what it means to be a man, Miss Payton? You don't meet men any more; they're all afraid of losing their jobs, afraid of spending a dollar, afraid of their own shadows. But not this man. No, sir. I don't lick anybody's boots. What are you staring at? This? It's an old custom of mine. Care to join me? No, I didn't think so.
(*He drinks from bottle*)

SYLVIA
Paul, don't; this isn't like you.

PAUL
How do you know what I'm like? How does anybody know? We all live alone, Miss Payton; we all live alone in a cruel and lonely world.
(*He drinks*)

SYLVIA
How true that is.

PAUL
You know what I'm going to do? Yes, sir. The hell with it. I'm dropping everything, leaving everything. The first bus

heading west tomorrow, you know who's going to be on it?
I am. You bet.
    (*He raises bottle to mouth*)

                    SYLVIA
    (*Tries to take bottle from him*)
Paul, you've had enough of that.

                    PAUL
    (*Pulls bottle away from her*)
Listen, this is no spur-of-the-minute thing with me, and it's not the whiskey doing the talking either. I've been thinking of it for a long long time. This city stinks for my money; there's nothing here but a lot of smoke, noise and corruption. I don't know where that bus is going to take me, but I'm not getting off until I find a place where there's plenty of fresh air, lots of room, that's what I want, lots of room, and mountains, mountains as high as you can see. Yes, sir. When I find that place I'm getting off and that's where I'm staying.

                    SYLVIA
I always dreamt of going somewhere like that, ever since I was a girl; some place away from everyone and everything I know.

                    PAUL
Do you mean that?

                    SYLVIA
I'd give anything.

PAUL
(Puts bottle on typewriter table)
Syl.

SYLVIA
Yes, Paul?

PAUL
Listen, we . . . we get along pretty well, don't we?

SYLVIA
We get along extremely well.

PAUL
(Standing behind her)
The times I thought of taking you in my arms and holding you . . .

SYLVIA
Oh, if you only had, Paul.

PAUL
It's not too late, is it?

SYLVIA
No, no, it's not.

PAUL
The two of us, together.
(He holds her about the waist; she clasps his hands)

SYLVIA

Oh, Paul. I'm so happy. I'll call my mother. And you call your wife. I don't want there to be any hard feelings. Let's make it as pleasant as possible for everyone.

PAUL

(*Stunned*)
You want me to call my wife?

SYLVIA

Of course, silly; we're getting married, aren't we?

PAUL

But you don't understand . . .

SYLVIA

We are getting married, aren't we?

PAUL

Aw, what's the use.

SYLVIA

I know; it's my fault; no matter what I do or say it's my fault.

PAUL

No, my fault; it's my fault. I'm no good, Sylvia. I never was. I never had the guts to do anything but feel sorry for myself. I've been a lazy selfish son-of-a-bitch all my life. I never did a damn thing that amounted to a bag of beans. And now . . . Oh, my God!
(*Leaning on typewriter, he sobs loudly*)

SYLVIA
Paul, stop it; what are you doing? What's wrong?

PAUL
I don't care for myself; it's not for me. My life's over. My wife . . .
    (*Shouting*)
That bitch can go to hell! But the kids, Sylvia. I love those kids. Now what's going to happen to them? I don't have a job; there's no money put away, nothing. What did I do? What was I trying to prove?

SYLVIA
Why don't you go in and speak to him? Apologize, tell him anything. You're one of the best typists he's ever had; don't forget that.

PAUL
Do you think there's a chance? I can type; no one can say I can't. That's one thing I can do. Look, Sylvia. Look.
    (*He stands with his back to the typewriter and with his hands behind him types*)
Check that. Go ahead. You'll find there isn't a single mistake. And this, look at this.
    (*He stands between both typewriters, spreads his arms out and types on both machines simultaneously*)

SYLVIA
I know, Paul; you're very good.

THE TYPISTS

PAUL
There. Perfect. Check it. Check it. And this, Sylvia, look at this.

SYLVIA
That's enough, Paul. I believe you. I know you can . . .
>   (*He stands on the chair at his typewriter, removes one shoe, gives it to* SYLVIA, *and types with his stockinged foot, swings carriage across with his large toe, then slumps down in chair*)

Come down from there. You are good, you're very good.

PAUL
They deserve everything I can give them, Syl. I love those kids.
>   (*He lifts up his foot;* SYLVIA *puts on his shoe*)

SYLVIA
I know. Now let's get you fixed up so you'll look presentable when you see him.
>   (*Straightens his tie, brushes his jacket, etc.*)

Stand still. Stop moving around.

PAUL
He'll never give me another chance, not after what I said to him.

SYLVIA
You just walk in and speak to him. There. Now you look fine. I'll fix things up out here. And we'd better get rid of this bottle.
>   (*She takes it away from him as he raises it to his mouth*)

PAUL

No more of that for me. I learned my lesson.

SYLVIA

I hope so. Well, go ahead in.

PAUL

Syl, I just want you to know this: if I get get my job back, you're going to see some changes. Paul Cunningham has grown up at last.

SYLVIA

Go ahead in.

PAUL

No, not until I thank you for . . . for everything you've done.

SYLVIA

I didn't do a thing.

PAUL

Yes you did; more than I can thank you for. Did you ever think, Syl, what would have happened if the two of us had met before I married Barbara?

SYLVIA

(*Wistfully*)
Yes, I thought of it, many times.

The Typists

PAUL
(*Moving toward her*)
Syl, listen to me . . .

SYLVIA
(*Raising her hands, moving away from him*)
Not that again. Please. Go in. Go on in.
(PAUL *exits to employer's office.* SYLVIA *empties whiskey bottle in drain of water cooler, then drops bottle into basket; she picks papers from floor; sits at typewriter, puts eyeglasses on, and types.* PAUL *enters. He is now in his fifties*)

PAUL
It's all right; it's all right. He's taken me back.

SYLVIA
I'm so glad for you.

PAUL
He was darn nice about it, too. He just listened to me and then he said, "It's understandable, Mr. Cunningham. We all have our problems."

SYLVIA
He can be nice when he wants to.

PAUL
"We all have our problems." He's not a stupid man.

SYLVIA
On the contrary, he understands a great many things.

The Typists

PAUL
You know, we should buy him something; a little gift from the staff, something to show our appreciation.
    (*Rubbing hands, sits at typewriter*)
Well, let's get to it. There's not much left to the day now.

SYLVIA
Yes, soon it'll be over.
    (*They type in silence. Suddenly* PAUL *breaks out in forced laughter*)

SYLVIA
What's so amusing?

PAUL
Miss Supervisor . . . I'll never forget that as long as I live. "Believe me, Mr. Cunningham, I didn't ask him to be made a supervisor. I don't like telling anyone what to do."

SYLVIA
We all have our pretensions, Paul.

PAUL
    (*Clearing his throat*)
That's very true.
    (*They type.* SYLVIA *starts to laugh*)

PAUL
What is it? What . . . what is it? What?

SYLVIA
I was just thinking of a boy I once went with.

THE TYPISTS

PAUL

The Chinese fellow?

SYLVIA

No, no. I don't know any Chinese fellow. This boy was an entertainer. He could make you laugh by just looking at you.

PAUL

Did I ever tell you, Sylvia, that I used to take singing lessons?

SYLVIA

No?

PAUL

I did. When I was eight, nine . . .

SYLVIA

(*Rises, collects typed cards*)
I didn't know that.

PAUL

(*Sings*)
Way down upon the Swanee River . . . Far, far from home . . .

SYLVIA

You do have a voice.

PAUL
(*Sings monosylabically*)
Da, *da,* da, da, da, *da, da* . . .

SYLVIA
(*At employer's door*)
Shh, not too loudly.
    (SYLVIA *exits, without tidying herself, to employer's office.* PAUL *types and sings monosylabically, using his typewriter as if it were a musical instrument. On the card he has just typed he notices an error, crumples it and slips it into his pocket; he continues singing.* SYLVIA *enters. They are now in their middle-sixties, aged, slow-moving, but not gray-wigged, not senile*)

PAUL
(*Looking at his watch*)
Sylvia, it's twelve minutes to five.

SYLVIA
We don't generally stop until ten minutes to, Paul.

PAUL
I know. But I thought . . .

SYLVIA
That wouldn't be fair.

PAUL
You're right, as always.
    (*They type*)

The Typists

PAUL
Now, Sylvia?
(*Without looking at timepiece*)

SYLVIA
There's still . . . I would say a minute.
(*They type*)

PAUL
Now, Sylvia?

SYLVIA
Yes . . . Now.

PAUL
Thank God.

SYLVIA
I am tired. A good hot bath and then to bed with me.
(*Rising he inadvertently brushes a card off the table; he picks it up, reads*)

PAUL
"All wool knickers. From factory to you. At a tremendous saving." Knickers. We've been selling knickers.

SYLVIA
(*Covering typewriters*)
Come, come, let's put everything away.

PAUL
(*Going to coat hanger*)
Not many people wear knickers nowadays, do they? Knick-

ers. They're warm, though; and practical, they're very practical.

SYLVIA
(As PAUL *struggles with his coat*)
Here, let me help you with that. Isn't it too early yet?

PAUL
Just getting ready.
(*He helps her put on her coat*)

SYLVIA
What time is it, Paul? It doesn't feel like five.

PAUL
(*Looking at wristwatch*)
Another . . . two minutes.
(*They sit down at typewriters, in their coats, immobile, expressionless, waiting for the two minutes to pass. Then* PAUL *looks at his watch*)

PAUL
(*Rising*)
It's time.

SYLVIA
(*As they move toward the employer's office*)
I have such a bad recollection. What is this new man's name, Paul?

THE TYPISTS

PAUL
Smith or Stone or . . . I never could remember names.

SYLVIA
We'll give him a friendly good-bye just the same.
(*They stand on the threshold of the office, wave and cry shrilly*)

PAUL
Good night. Good night in there.

SYLVIA
Have a pleasant evening. Good night.

PAUL
I'll walk you to the subway, Sylvia.

SYLVIA
That would be very nice.
(SYLVIA *stands by the door, buttoning her coat.* PAUL *removes some crumpled cards from his pocket, he looks at them, forlornly, let's them fall from his hands to the floor. He starts toward* SYLVIA *but changes his mind, returns, gets down on his haunches and picks up some crumpled cards; he looks around the office for a place to put them; finding none he slips them back into his pockets and exits with* SYLVIA)

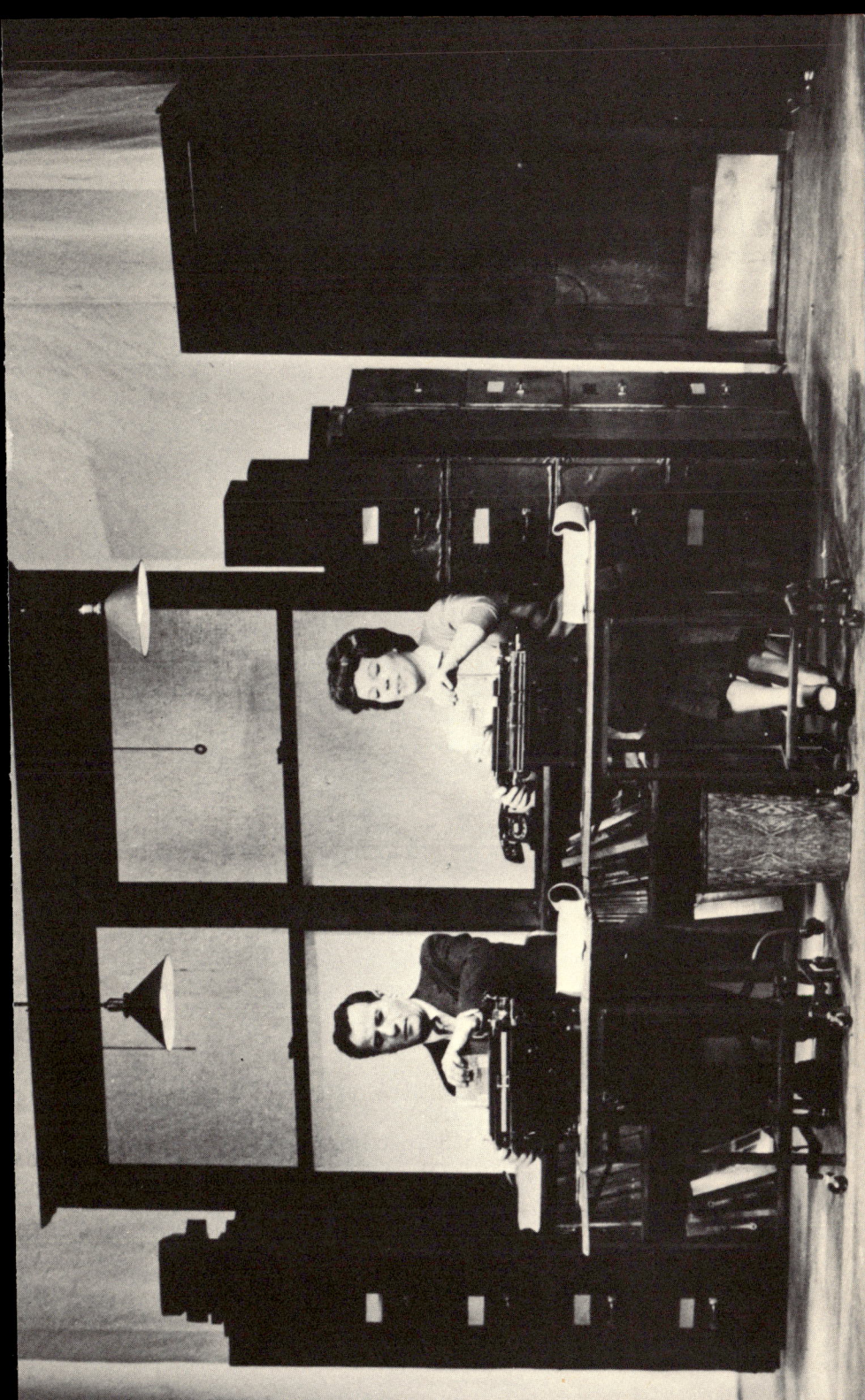

The Tiger

THE SCENE:
A basement room, dingy, cluttered, stacks of books lying about. On the left a short flight of steps and a door leading into the street. Next to the steps is a bureau on which there is a plant and more books. In the rear a cot, a lamp, a phonograph on a small table; running over the cot is a string of laundry. Against the right wall, at an angle, is a door to the kitchen, on the door is a blackboard—the words: TODAY'S WORD, SYMBIOSIS *are written on the blackboard. Forward, left, a wooden chair; right, a frayed bulky upholstered chair. Red water pipes cross the ceiling and come down at both sides of the room.*

Flashes of lightning break the darkness. Thunder, the sound of heavy rain.

The door is suddenly thrown open. BEN *enters, carrying* GLORIA *over his shoulder, like a sack; his raincoat is tied around the upper part of her body.*

      GLORIA
  (*Muffled voice; kicking her legs*)
For your own sake . . . Put me down. Put me down . . .

BEN

(*Carries her across to bed*)

Stop it! Stop it! Do you think I'm playing games with you? Is that what you think? Ha! That's a laugh. This is strength you're feeling on your bones, lady, primitive, animal strength. There's no arguing with that. Oh, no.

(GLORIA *is seated on edge of bed;* BEN *turns on lamp*)

Now you stay there. Don't move. Don't budge an inch. I'll be right with you. In a minute . . . In a minute . . .

(*He runs to door, closes it, pulls curtains over small window above bureau.* GLORIA *rises, moves blindly about the room.* BEN *grabs her, drags her to the wooden chair*)

Come back. Come back here.

(*He ties her wrists behind the chair with the belt of his raincoat*)

GLORIA

(*Muffled voice*)

What are you doing? Take this off. Please. I can't breathe under here, I can't . . .

BEN

Scream; scream all you want. You have my permission. It's not going to help you, though. Not here, it won't. We're quite alone. Quite, quite alone. No conditions. I insist on that. I don't accept conditions of any kind. That's a point for you to keep in mind.

(*She is tied to chair; he moves around to face her*)

There. That's it. Each of us in his proper place.

(*Removes raincoat from her*)

You like flirting, don't you, lady? Do anything for a good time. I had those propositions before. Don't make any mistake about that.
(*He takes towel from line, wipes his face*)

GLORIA

But I never flirted with you. I didn't. I swear, that's the truth. This is silly. Please, let me go.

BEN

Go? Let you go? After all that trouble of dragging you through those back alleys? After getting my new pants wet? Oh, no. Not a chance. Not tonight, lady. I've got something else in mind for you.

GLORIA

I don't know what you want; really, I don't. But I won't tell anyone anything. I promise. So far as I'm concerned none of this ever happened. I didn't see you. I kept my eyes closed. Look. They're still closed. I have no idea what you look like. Just let me go. Please, let me go . . .
(*She sobs*)

BEN

(*Sits on steps, removes shoes, wet socks, takes pair of socks from bureau, puts them on; shoes remain off*)
Cry. Yes. Cry. Your tears are beautiful. I can watch you all night. It's as natural for you to cry as it is for the tiger to stalk its prey and gorge itself. Cry. Go ahead. Human history is filled with countless relevant examples.

The Tiger

GLORIA

Why did you take me? Why out of everybody did you have to take me?

BEN

Things are what they have to be, that's why they are. You don't get it, do you? I stood in the doorway of that decrepit stationery store for three hours, for more than three hours, who knows how many. I let six, seven, eight of you go by, and then you came click-clacking along in those high-heeled shoes of yours, and I knew you were the one, it was you. At first I had a . . . a almost uncontrollable impulse to finish you off right there. Finish you off and be done with it. But when I touched you, when my fingers grabbed hold of you, a voice deep inside of me said, "No. Don't. Wait. Take her. Let it be something special and . . . and sacred even. A ritual, a ritual of . . ."

GLORIA

You're not that inhuman.

BEN

That human! That human!
   (*Hangs wet socks on line; in despair*)
Nobody understands. Not even Schopenhauer or . . . or Nietzsche. They always have that carrot dangling in front of your nose. Be more than you are, be more than human, transcend, go above, beyond, up, up, up . . .
   (*At blackboard*)
But no! That isn't it. I say, be less than you are. To be what you are.
   (*Draws a descending line*)

Be less! less! less! than you are.
(*Erases blackboard*)

GLORIA

I can't talk to you. You're . . .

BEN

I'm what?

GLORIA

Nothing. Nothing.

BEN

Insane? Is that what you wanted to say? Insane?
(*Paces around her chair*)
I hope so. Oh, God. I hope so. I am insane, right? You wanted to say it. I didn't tell you. I didn't influence that remark. But you knew; you sensed it. I agree with your judgment. Emphatically. You don't meet people like me every day, people with my ideas, with the courage of my convictions. I am insane, say it!

GLORIA

If you'd listen to me . . .

BEN

Not until I give you permission! Is that clear? Between us, between you and me, there's only one thing that counts. Power, strength, my physical superiority, this fist and this arm. Here, tonight, I say to you I am insane so that I can be human. You see how great it is? You see how everything

THE TIGER

falls into place? You don't understand anything, do you? Linguistic concepts are too much for your little female birdbrain. But that's all right. You have other assets. You're nice to touch, I assume. You're soft. Your blood is warm and alive.

> (*He tries to kiss her. She moves her head away. He presses his nose to her cheek*)

Now? Do I end your miserable life now? Quickly and suddenly . . .

> (*Looks about*)

All right. All right.

> (*Takes record out of album-cover, puts it on phonograph: music, Tschaikovsky's Concerto No. 1*)

We'll do it. You sit there. Right there. We'll do it now and we'll do it properly. With all the trimmings. With all . . .

> (*She turns her head back towards him. He kisses her, daintily, on the cheek, then shuts phonograph*)

That was a little better. Sometimes the tiger has to claw the tigress; then she understands what it's all about.

GLORIA

Let me tell you . . .

BEN

Did I give you permission to speak? Did I?

GLORIA

May I have your permission?

BEN

All right. You're learning. You can speak to me now if you wish.

The Tiger

GLORIA
I . . . I'm a married woman. I have been married for the last six years. My husband is an . . . honest hard-working man. We have our own home; it isn't fully paid. We're not what you'd call well-off by any means. We have two small children, two little girls. And you can ask anyone out on the Island where we . . .

BEN
Enough! Enough of that noise! I don't like babbling women. You can cry, but don't babble. Is that clear? Any woman who leaves her kids to go tramping around at night is a whore and she deserves, ipso facto, what she gets.

GLORIA
I wasn't . .

BEN
What?

GLORIA
Can I please say something?

BEN
All right, now.

GLORIA
I wasn't tramping around all night. I wasn't. Every Thursday . . . I belong to a bridge club and a few other girls whom I worked with when I was single . . . It all goes to charity!

BEN
Continue. I didn't say stop, did I?

GLORIA
It's only one night a week. I'm in every other night. I get out so little, that when I get the chance . . .

BEN
(*Stands behind her, strokes her hair, gently*)
Your husband takes you out on Saturdays. All husbands take their wives out on Saturdays.

GLORIA
Not for some time now. I swear to you, that's the truth. He's so tired when the weekend comes and . . . It costs so much for a baby-sitter, even if you can get someone . . . reliable. Please, don't.

BEN
(*Facing her*)
I want you to kiss me.

GLORIA
No, no . . .

BEN
I said I want you to kiss me.

GLORIA
I can't, please . . .
(*She lowers her head*)

BEN

Pick up your head! Pick it up!
 (*She raises her head; without kissing her*)
I'll accept that for now. But you'd better learn and learn quickly. I'm not to be contradicted. Not in word, thought or deed. I'm all your world tonight. Remember that, lady.

GLORIA

I won't ask you to consider what you're doing for myself. It isn't myself I'm concerned with right now. But I do have a husband and a family. All of them will suffer. It's not only me. Why don't you consider them? Why don't you . . .

BEN

I didn't hear a word you said because . . .
 (*Flaring petulantly*)
because you didn't have my permission to speak! You can cry whenever you want, however. That much I allow you because you're a woman.

GLORIA

I'm not going to cry. There's no reason to cry. I believe that there's goodness in you. I can see it in your eyes. Isn't there someone whom you love very much?

BEN

Besides myself?

GLORIA

Besides yourself.

The Tiger

BEN

No one.

GLORIA

There must be someone. Your mother . . .

BEN

Don't make me laugh.

GLORIA

A wife?

BEN

Do you think I'm that dumb?

GLORIA

Then friends. You must have had friends.

BEN

No one. No one. I have no one but myself and that's all that counts. Me. Myself. The fulfillment of my own body and my own primitive soul. Sometimes . . . Sometimes I walk along the street at night and my feet, as I walk, my feet feel like large soft paws, and the moon, the moon shining overhead, so brightly, so primeval, I want to raise my head and . . . and let loose from inside of me some wild strange . . . a sound that hasn't been heard for thousands of years, but it's inside of us, you see, deep, deep inside of us . . . Tonight I don't have to hold anything in. Tonight I have you. To play with. To destroy. To do whatever I want with. After that, I don't care. I want you to kiss me. Now.

GLORIA
You're driving me out of my mind.

BEN
You don't want to?
  (*She does, on his cheek*)
Not good enough!

GLORIA
Leave me alone, leave me alone . . .

BEN
  (*Turns on phonograph: music*)
All right, prepare yourself! We don't have to speak any more. We'll be quiet and still and listen to our heartbeats, pounding, pounding . . . That which is deepest in us will rise, will overcome us in a moment of blind primitive passion . . . Then we will be ourselves, the essence, the primal force, free of all hypocrisy, free of all pretending, pretending to morality, pretending to sanity, pretending . . .
  (GLORIA *kisses him lightly*)
Unsatisfactory. You will hold your lips to mine until I give you the signal. Now.
  (*He snaps his fingers. She kisses him. He shuts phonograph*)
Better. There are signs of progress. I'm glad to see that some learning is taking place.

GLORIA
My arms are sore. Can't you untie me?

BEN
Did you speak?

GLORIA
I . . . I didn't mean to. Can I ask you a favor?

BEN
(*Erases board; absent-mindedly*)
Was it you who wanted to say something?

GLORIA
I have a favor to ask of you.

BEN
(*Reluctantly*)
All right. Go ahead.

GLORIA
The blood isn't circulating in my arms. I'd really appreciate it if you untied me. I won't try to get away.

BEN
I don't believe you. Not for a single solitary minute do I believe you. But . . . I have no objection. Tonight the word fear is in your vocabulary, not mine.
(*He unties her*)
Of course you realize that if you do try to get away I'll have to punish you. Maybe even kill you, right here on the spot! You can never tell when I'll lose control of myself. So be careful!
(*Pulls threateningly on raincoat belt*)

GLORIA
Thank you. You see, there is good in you. You can be reasonable.

BEN

Take off that skirt.

GLORIA

Isn't there any way I can convince you.

BEN

No. Do as I say.
    (*He snaps belt in air*)
Do you hear me?
    (*She removes her skirt, stands in loud garish slip*)
Nice. Very, very nice. Let me have it. Now sit down in that chair. Go ahead.
    (*She sits on wooden chair. He looks at skirt, puts it on bureau. He then takes cigarette and matches from bureau, lights cigarette and sits down on steps*)

GLORIA

May I have one?

BEN

No.

GLORIA

It's cold here. I'm freezing.
    (*He ignores her*)
You could make yourself some easy money if you just let me go. My husband would gladly give it to you. Why don't you phone him? You can ask for . . . five, ten thousand dollars. He can get it. Wouldn't you be better off with all that money?

THE TIGER

BEN

A man lives in his mind, not in a place. No use explaining it to you. I'd be wasting my time. Idiots. A world of idiots and illiterates, too damn dense to comprehend the most basic laws governing their own existence. What does the name of Plato mean to them? Or Beethoven or Spinoza or Rembrandt? Idiots. You all follow one another like a pack of sheep, one following the other . . . Up at nine, out of the house, into the subway, down the street, work until twelve, lunch, everybody eating, over the counter, munch, munch, munch . . . chock-full-a-nuts, munch, munch, munch, back at one, work until five, down the street, into the subway, out of the subway, into the house, in bed at ten . . . Sheep, millions of sheep.

GLORIA

Out on the Island where I live . . .

BEN

Did I ask your opinion?

GLORIA

I wanted to say . . .

BEN

I'm not interested in what you wanted to say. I'm not giving lessons in democratic principles. Not this semester, lady.
   (*Rises*)
Everybody has something to say; everybody has an opinion to give you. But do they have the background, the training, the mental discipline, to give you an opinion on the facts?

[88

On objectivity? On scientific comprehension? Oh, no. Not that. But they all babble. Right?

GLORIA

Yes.

BEN

You think I'm right?

GLORIA

Yes, I do. I agree with you.

BEN

What was I right about? Do you know? Do you fathom the implications, the ramifications?
  (*At blackboard, writes* A, B, C)
Reiterate my line of reasoning and present me with a brief summation of its salient points. Begin, now.

GLORIA

I couldn't . . .

BEN

I said, begin, now! This minute, begin!

GLORIA

I'll try. I think what you were saying is that in a democracy where everybody has a voice in the government, despite intelligence, despite ability, this leads to the false belief . . .

BEN

  (*Erases board, quickly, angrily*)
Is that what you think?

THE TIGER

GLORIA
Isn't it ..

BEN
Who wrote *The Divine Comedy*?

GLORIA
Dante?

BEN
When was the Civil War?

GLORIA
Between 1861 and 1865.

BEN
How do you spell concatenation?

GLORIA
Concatenation. C-O-N-C-A-T-E-N-A-T-I-O-N. How do you spell pulchritude?

BEN
Pulchritude. Capital P-U-L-C-H-R-I-T-U-D-E. Physiology.

GLORIA
Physiology. P-H-Y-S-I-O-L-O-G-Y. Somnambulism.

BEN
Somnambulism. Capital S-O-M-N-A-M-B-U-L-I-S-M. Miscegenation.

GLORIA
Miscegenation. M-I-C-S . . .

BEN
M-I-S-C . . .
>(*Writes S C, S C on blackboard*)

S-C! S-C! E-G-E-N-A-T-I-O-N. You stupid bird-brain. Don't you dare speak loosely to me. Not unless you're willing to pay the consequences.
>(*Wagging finger*)

That's a point for you to keep in mind.
>(*Erases board*)

GLORIA
I will. In the future. I will. May I . . . please have a glass of water?

BEN
I'm not your servant. Maybe tomorrow, but not tonight. Oh, no. Not tonight, lady.

GLORIA
I'll get it, if . . .

BEN
Ahh, sit there and shut up.
>(BEN *goes into kitchen, closing door behind him.* GLORIA *rises, picks up her pocketbook, skirt, starts moving up the steps. At once the entrance door is thrown open and* BEN *enters, holding a glass of water.* GLORIA *jumps back in fright*)

THE TIGER

BEN

You going someplace?

GLORIA

No, I was just . . .

BEN

Never mind you were just. I know what you were just.
    (*He empties glass of water contemptuously into plant*)
You can try those tricks on your husband, but not with me. Is that clear? I know what goes on, all right. You're all the same. Every damn one of you.
    (*Touches wet feet with annoyance*)
You wait until they go off to work and then it's first come, first served. You ask them in for a cup of coffee; tell them there's no hurry . . . Oh, no. There's no hurry. There's no one at home, you make sure they know that. I had those propositions before, plenty of times.

GLORIA

I've never been untrue to my husband, never. I swear to you.

BEN

    (*Points*)
Get back to your chair.

GLORIA

    (*On wooden chair*)
I won't try to leave again. Really. I'd like a cigarette, please.

BEN
(*Takes socks from bureau*)
I'm running out of socks, damn it! If you try anything, it'll be the last time. I hope you had enough education to understand that. You did go to school, didn't you?
(*Sits on steps, puts on dry pair of socks*)

GLORIA
You probably won't believe it, but I graduated from college. So did my husband. That's where we met. We were both taking the same course. He . . . sat right next to me.

BEN
That explains your ignorance, thoroughly and completely. I remember once I walked into a class at some stupid college uptown. I thought I would listen to the wisdom of the ages, the prophets speaking through the intelligent and refined mind of a scholar, a pedant.
(*Rises*)
There was a young cockeyed kid standing on a high platform. He had one hand in his pocket; the other hand he was waving in the air as if he was leading a band. "The packaging of an article cannot be circumscribed, ladies and gentlemen, by a few simple rules. We must here consider not only the item which is to be packaged, but the conditions under which it must be sold, the costs involved, the packaging prevalent on the market, motivating the buyer, satisfying the producer, complying with state and federal regulations . . ."
(*Laughing*)

THE TIGER

I started laughing like crazy. I couldn't help myself. I had to put a handkerchief over my face and stagger out of there.
    (*Grimly*)
That was as far as I got in college.
    (*Hangs wet socks on line*)

GLORIA

You mean you're not a graduate?

BEN

Did I tell you I was?

GLORIA

No, of course not. But . . . your vocabulary, the way you talk . . . I was almost certain . .

BEN

College is for imbeciles, for sheep, for baa baa sheep. I taught myself everything I know.
    (*Lifts armful of books from floor*)
By reading, by studying, by perusing the prophets, the philosophers, the anthropologists, the poets, the scientists. Every night I read, whatever I could lay my hands on, years and years of reading and studying until . . . until I gave myself a diploma: it was a doctorate in comprehensive ontology.
    (*Puts books on floor*)
I understood then, I saw through the lies and hypocrisy; the truth was as clear to me as a ball of crystal. They wanted

to dehumanize me, yes, yes, precisely that; they wanted to make a sheep of me, a baa baa sheep. That . . . That which was purest in me, the animal savage, innocent, primitive, childlike, that I had to save, I had to salvage and redeem; and it's for that, for the right to be human as I must be to live, that I offer you in sacrifice on this evening of May the 22nd.

GLORIA

Does it have to be a living human being?

BEN

You poor bird-brain. You poor ignorant bird-brain. What do you know about being? Being? Ha! What do you know about your own body, about the elementary physical processes of your own body? For example. Did you ever ask yourself why you're so small there?
 (*Points at her breasts*)

GLORIA

(*Looking down*)
Small? Where?

BEN

There! There! Right where you're looking. The mammalian glands. Your mother was small, too, I bet. Hereditary. Genetic evolution. A fascinating field. Fascinating. Darwin, Lysenko, Dobzansky . . . In a hundred years you won't have any. There won't be any. Nobody'll have any. That's right.
 (*Outlines on blackboard*)

The Tiger

The giraffe's neck, number one; the monkey's tail, number two.
    (*Turning*)
Those things are going to disappear. Like that.
    (*Snaps fingers*)
How does it happen? Lysenko! That's how. But you wouldn't know anything about that.
    (*Erases board*)

          GLORIA

I'm interested in it. For a number of years I subscribed to one of the science magazines, and each month they'd have articles on a particular branch of science, say, biology or . . .

          BEN

Let me have your shoes.

          GLORIA

My shoes?

          BEN

Did you hear me?

          GLORIA

Why do you want my shoes?
    (*Gives them to him*)

          BEN

We come closer and closer to the end which is the beginning. The beginning is in the end and the end is in the beginning. Time is like an egg and life . . . life is like a chicken that lays the egg.

GLORIA

Is . . . Is that original?

BEN

What do you think it is?

GLORIA

I like it. I do.

BEN
(*Sits in upholstered chair*)
Nights and nights alone in here, studying, reading the masters, looking deep, deep inside myself . . .

GLORIA

Despite everything, I can't help enjoy listening to you. Before I married, you know, I was a social worker with the Department of Welfare. It was part of my job to direct people into work they were suited for, temperamentally, educationally . . . It was very absorbing work. I really hated to leave. But . . . Why didn't you go to college? I think you could have made a very good instructor.

BEN

At one time that was my ambition. To teach in college. To be a professor of epistemology and linguistics. Those bastards. They're not worth spitting on. I don't need them. I don't need anybody!

THE TIGER

GLORIA

What happened?

BEN

Did I give you permission to speak?
(*Pause*)
I failed the damn entrance exam. I . . . I can't speak French and they don't take you unless you can speak French or some damn language.
(*Almost bawling*)
Oh, I tried, I tried. But I couldn't do it. I couldn't. Go ahead. Laugh. Is that what you feel like doing?

GLORIA

Not in the least. I just can't understand it. It shouldn't have been difficult for you.

BEN

(*Takes books from bureau drawer, gives them to her*)
See all these books? French books. I took courses in it, studied it with tutors, with Frenchmen, with whoever I could find. It wouldn't sink in. Call it an emotional block. Call it whatever the hell you want. I don't give a damn any more for that crap. I have other ambitions now. More important things to do. Life, that's what counts. Not degrees or accomplishments or being sucked in. I don't accept it. Do you hear me? I don't accept it!

GLORIA

But it isn't too late. You still can do it.

[98

BEN
What are you talking about? Do you know how old I am?

GLORIA
I'd say thirty-six, thirty-seven.

BEN
Forty-two in August. No. I'm not interested any more.

GLORIA
But forty-two isn't old; that's where you're so wrong. You're in the prime of life and isn't that the time to get an education?

BEN
Are you deaf? I told you they wouldn't take me.

GLORIA
Only because you didn't know French. I remember the trouble I had passing my French exams.

BEN
You speak French?

GLORIA
(*Coyly; as is*)
Oui, un petit.
  (BEN *rises, angrily takes books from her and dumps them into bureau drawer*)

THE TIGER

BEN
Get back to your chair. Get back . . .

GLORIA
I'm in my chair. This is my chair!

BEN
Not that chair.
(*Points to upholstered chair*)
That chair! That chair! Get over there. Go ahead. I don't want to hear another word out of you, understand? I want silence, complete and utter silence.
(GLORIA *is reseated.* BEN *removes jacket*)
If I lose control of myself, you're the one who's going to pay for it. So be careful. I'm warning you. Too much damn talking anyway. Everybody has something to say. But do they know (*Indifferently, he presses his hand on the hot-water pipe, pulls it away with an inaudible howl, wags it furiously*) what they say? Do they care? They babble. They don't talk to one another. Oh, no. They talk to themselves. They talk to their own egos.

GLORIA
That is perceptive of you. There's no communication between people any more.

BEN
Did I tell you to shut up? Listen. You might learn something.
(*Slight pause*)
There's no communication between people any more. Ev-

[100

erybody's inside of himself, inside in his own little egotistical shell. You meet somebody in the street, they say "How are you?" Do you think they care how you are? Do you think they care? Ha! That's a laugh. It just comes out of their mouths, drivels out; there's no feelings, no interest, no humanity, nothing. "How are you?" Ha! What a mockery. What a deceit. You say, "Oh, I'm fine." And they don't even listen.

GLORIA

They don't listen.

BEN

That's what gets me. They ask the question, "How are you?" And when you answer them, when you say, "I'm fine," they don't even listen; they don't care. I know. I see what's happening. A couple of days ago I met this kid who works in the A & P where I buy my things. He stopped me and said, "How are you?" By the time I could say, "I'm fine," he was on the crosstown bus, three blocks down the street!

GLORIA

They're all alike. They're not concerned with human values, only with making money, with keeping up with the Joneses.

BEN

Are you going to shut up? I said I want silence from you, complete and utter silence!
  (*Slight pause*)
They're not concerned with human values, only with keep-

ing up with the Joneses, with grabbing as much as they can get their hands on. That's all they think about. Money, the bitch-goddess! They're all after it.

GLORIA

But what matters, finding one's identity, that they don't care about. That's why there are no individuals today.

BEN

(*Sitting down*)
That's right.

GLORIA

Everybody wears the same clothes, does the same kind of work, talks about the same subjects . . .

BEN

It's as if they were all coming out of Detroit on the assembly line.

GLORIA

You couldn't have put it better. That's precisely what all this talk on conformity is.

BEN

I know. I know. You don't have to tell me. It's getting so bad people are beginning to resemble one another. I mean, actually, physically resemble one another. You think I'm kidding? You walk along the street any day in the week and try to get somebody's attention. Try it. Go ahead. They don't look at you. They don't want to look at you. Stick your head right under their noses and they still won't look at you. Why should they? You look just like everybody else!

GLORIA

I couldn't contradict you. I see it with my own eyes.

BEN

(*Rises*)
I've been living in this place for seven years, seven years! Do you know what the landlady said to me when I went up to pay her the rent last time? "Sorry. No vacancies."

GLORIA

She didn't know you.

BEN

After seven years. But that's not all of it. Do you know what happened to me tonight? Listen to this. I walked into a restaurant to get something to eat when this woman with a man's hat on her head, get that, a man's hat on her head, I never saw her before in my life . . . This woman grabbed my arm and said, "You son-of-a-bitch, you're late!" I said, "Lady, what are you talking about?" She said, "You know damn well what I'm talking about. Come on home, you little piss-pot, I want to get you home; come on . . ." She kept pulling at my arm and . . . Look.
  (*Brings her his raincoat, shows her the sleeve*)
Look what she did. Tore my raincoat.

GLORIA

Oh, that's awful. That is awful.

THE TIGER

BEN

She kept pulling at my arm and hitting me over the head with her damn pocketbook. There was a whole crowd watching us. I don't know how the hell I got away from her. And I still didn't have anything to eat.

GLORIA

She must have been drunk.

BEN

Drunk or crazy, what difference does it make? The point is that everybody's beginning to resemble one another. That's what we're up against. Read your Mendel. Read your history books on the Industrial Revolution. It's all there. It's no secret. Try to live in this world. Go ahead. Try.

GLORIA

It's becoming impossible. I know.

BEN

(*Seated*)
Impossible. That's just the word. And what do you think'll happen once this population explosion we're having gets moving, huh? Can you imagine what it's going to be like with three million people standing at the bus stop, all looking the same, all wearing the same hat and coat!

GLORIA

We won't even be able to use umbrellas.

BEN
You bet we won't.

GLORIA
Nobody listens.

BEN
Chaos. It'll be sheer chaos.

GLORIA
But does anybody listen?

BEN
Millions and millions of people; millions of sheep.

GLORIA
Nobody listens.

BEN
What?

GLORIA
I said nobody listens.

BEN
You put your finger right on it.

GLORIA
That's how it is. When it's too late, then they'll decide to do something about it.

BEN

I don't know. And they accept it. That's what gets me. They accept it.

    (As she talks GLORIA rises, picks up her pocketbook, returns to upholstered chair; she takes a cigarette out and then discovers that she has no matches; she goes to bureau, picks up a book of matches, returns to chair, lights a cigarette)

GLORIA

Out on the Island where I live, that's where you really see what's happening. It's unbelievable the extent to which they all live the same dreary lives, doing the same dull things. I've seen it grow; and it gets worse and worse. People when they first move into the neighborhood always seem interested in a great many things and they seem to have a great many interests. But after six months . . . All they can talk about is crab grass and bowling and what somebody else's wife is doing. That's where the danger is. It's not so much that we're all going to look alike; after all, that's only physical, but that we're all going to think alike and have the same social attitudes—that's something to keep in mind, the same social attitudes. And right there is where the real danger is.

BEN

You're telling me? Listen, lady, I've been fighting it for years!

GLORIA

(*Seated*)

You should fight it. We all should fight it. That's why our hospitals are filled with people who absolutely cannot function on any level. Do you know how many beds there are in our hospitals for each patient that needs a bed? You wouldn't believe it if I told you. But there are statistics that prove, conclusively, that in some hospitals there are three patients for every bed. Three patients for every bed. Think about it a minute. And it'll get worse and worse and nobody'll do anything about it. At least nearly nobody. The girls with whom I play bridge, we had raffle books printed and what we're doing is trying to get as many beds into these hospitals as we can; make every effort to get each patient a bed.

(*Removes raffle book from pocketbook; rises*)

It's only one dollar a raffle or a book of twenty raffles for nineteen dollars.

(*A pause as she holds out raffle book;* BEN *stares dumbly at her*)

You . . . You can win a television set or an AM/FM radio or . . . or a vacuum cleaner . . .

BEN

(*Another pause; then with sudden fervor; rises*)

And what about the atomic bomb, huh? What about the atomic bomb? You think they know what they're doing? Those lunatics don't know from one minute to the next what they're doing. But don't say anything. Don't do anything. Let them blow us all up. What the hell, we don't count. There's a million more where we came from.

THE TIGER

GLORIA

I never trusted any of them.

BEN

Two thousand years of civilization, two thousand years, and the only way we can survive is by digging holes in the ground and living like the lowest specie of insect life.

GLORIA

So long as they talk of what's happening in outer space and all the great progress we're supposed to be making.

BEN

Outer space. Outer space. Up theirs with outer space. What about us down here?

GLORIA

They must think we're all a bunch of fools. I had an argument with someone about this: he was so certain we have nothing to worry about. But try to argue with someone while he's pulling out crab grass. It's a joke out there. Everything's a joke.

BEN

It's that bad, huh?

GLORIA

You don't know the half of it. Most of the time I don't know what to do with myself. There's no one I can really talk to. And as for intellectual excitement or appreciation of the arts . . . It's another world. I have to come to the city just for a breath of fresh air.

BEN
I couldn't live anywhere else myself.

GLORIA
We had a place downtown for a few years but we had to plan for when the children were ready for school . . . You know how the schools are in the city.

BEN
Idiots. The whole system's filled with idiots.

GLORIA
They're driving out the middle-class, that's what they're doing.

BEN
Ahh, what's the use of talking?

GLORIA
(*Seated in upholstered chair*)
It helps. It does. It's good to talk about these things.
    (*Slight pause*)
You are making a mistake, you know. I can teach you French. There's no reason why you shouldn't . . .

BEN
Are you deaf? I told you it's too late.

GLORIA
But it's not too late. It's really not.

BEN
Like hell it isn't. Do you know how old I am?

GLORIA
I'd say . . . forty-two.

BEN
That's right. How did you know?

GLORIA
Because I know people. I know you and I know what you're capable of. Look. Sit down. We have time, don't we? There's no hurry. My husband goes to bed at nine. He never waits up for me and he never knows when I get in. What book do you want to use?
>   (*Takes book from bureau drawer; returns to upholstered chair*)

This one looks as if it'll do. We'll try it. Sit down. Please. We'll start at the beginning.
>   (*Pulls wooden chair closer; reads first-year French, badly*)

Bonjour, monsieur.
>   (*No response*)

Are you going to do it with me or not?

BEN
(Sits on wooden chair; reads, unenthusiastically)
Bonjour, mademoiselle.

GLORIA
Very good. That was very good. Je m'appelle Gloria. Comment vous appelez-vous?

BEN
Je m'appelle Benjamin.

GLORIA
No, not quite; hold your lips like this and let the words run into each other. Like this. Je m'appelle Benjamin. Try it.

BEN
Je m'appelle Benjamin.

GLORIA
Now you have it.
(Reads)
Comment allez-vous, monsieur?

BEN
(Reads)
Très bien, merci; et vous?

GLORIA
Pas trop mal, merci; mais mon frère est malade.

THE TIGER

BEN
C'est dommage. Je regrette beaucoup.

GLORIA
Wonderful. That was really wonderful.

BEN
It didn't sound bad, did it?

GLORIA
Bad? It was absolutely perfect. Why, we sounded just like a French couple sitting in their home and chatting. You must have been joking when you said you couldn't learn French.

BEN
It seems a lot easier now but . . .
    (*Rises*)
What the hell are we doing? Do you know how I live? How I support myself? I'm a postman, a letter carrier.
    (*Enters kitchen, returns with bag of tangerines, offers one to* GLORIA; *they are both seated, eating tangerines*)
I go from door to door, ringing bells and opening mailboxes. Me, with what I know, with my education. Okay, so that's it. That's all I'm good for. They say so. They lay down the law. This is what you are. This is how you have to spend your life. Oh, no. I don't accept it. I don't accept those conditions.

The Tiger

GLORIA

It's criminal, that's what it is. Just look how far you've gone, with no one's help, through your own efforts. It would be a pity if you gave everything up now. I know you could be an instructor, there isn't a doubt in my mind. Try. It's for your own good, you know.

BEN

It's not as simple as you're making it.

GLORIA

I'm not saying it's simple, but why should you have to suffer because you have the courage to live your own life, without compromising, without accepting the lies? When I think of the people who are able to get ahead nowadays . .

BEN

You don't have to tell me. But that's what they want, that's what they've geared the whole stupid society to.

GLORIA

It makes my blood boil.

BEN

Just because they've got a college degree or know how to wear those tight faggot pants . . . You wait. Russia's going to crush us like a bunch of ants if we don't wise up.

GLORIA

You don't know how right you are. My own husband, he has absolutely no talent in anything. I don't think he's ever

said or done an original thing. And as for reading a book
. . . Just try to get him to read a book. I tell you, if not
for the children . . . But that's another story. Do you
know what he is? Listen to this. An assistant executive, he's
an assistant executive in one of the largest textile factories
in the city, and he makes every year—wait till you hear
this, twelve thousand dollars for sitting behind a desk and
cutting Kewpie dolls out of scraps of material.

BEN

I bet he's a college graduate.

GLORIA

Do you know why? I watched him. I know. He used to sit
in his seat all during the lecture, hardly moving, every muscle in his face absolutely rigid. He'd stare up at the instructor with wide-open eyes, as if he was listening to a sermon,
but there were earplugs in his ears; he hates listening to
anyone but himself. At the end of each lecture he'd go up
to the instructor and say, "My name is William Hamlin. I
want you to know, Professor, that your lecture tonight was
one of the most brilliant I ever heard."

BEN

They're not interested in the person, not in what the individual can do. All they want to know is how many years
did you take this course, how many points do you have in
this subject or that subject. You need twelve points in social
psychology to become a supervisor in the post office. I
couldn't even get that!

GLORIA
Then go for your degree, Ben. Prove to them that you're a lot better and a lot smarter than any of them. You can do it.

BEN
What makes you so damn sure?

GLORIA
Because I have confidence in you.

BEN
Do you mean that?

GLORIA
(*Softly*)
I do, Ben.
(*After exchanging glances, holds out book, reads*)
Bonsoir, monsieur.

BEN
(*Reads, eagerly*)
Comment vous portez-vous ce soir?

GLORIA
Good. Je me porte très bien, merci.

BEN
Comment va votre soeur?

GLORIA
(*Corrects him*)
Comment va votre soeur?

THE TIGER

                        BEN
Comment va votre soeur?

                      GLORIA
    (*Nods*)
Elle a mal à la tête.

                        BEN
C'est très désagréable.

                      GLORIA
Excellent. That was excellent, Ben.

                        BEN
    (*Stares intently at her, not from book*)
Mademoiselle?

                      GLORIA
    (*Puts book aside*)
Monsieur?

                        BEN
Comment vous appelez-vous?

                      GLORIA
Je m'appelle Gloria, monsieur; et vous?

                        BEN
Je m'appelle Benjamin.

                      GLORIA
Comment allez-vous, Monsieur Benjamin?

BEN
Très bien, merci; et vous?

GLORIA
Très bien.

BEN
(*Touches her shoulder, uncertainly*)
Mademoiselle . . .

GLORIA
(*Rising, coyly*)
Monsieur?

BEN
(*Rising, heatedly*)
Mademoiselle.

GLORIA
(*Melting*)
Monsieur.

BEN
(*Hugging her*)
Oh, mademoiselle, ma chérie, mademoiselle . .

GLORIA
(*Embracing him*)
Monsieur; mon magnifique monsieur.

BEN
(*Lifts her off her feet, carries her to bed, jubilantly*)
Oh, mademoiselle, ma chérie, ma chérie . . .

GLORIA
(*Kicking her feet, playfully protesting*)
Oh, non, non, non, non. Non, monsieur. Monsieur . . .

BEN
Oui, mademoiselle. Oui. Oui. Oui. Oui . . .
    (GLORIA *pulls cord of lamp, turning out light, throwing bed in darkness. Unseen,* BEN *turns on the phonograph: the main theme of Tchaikovsky's Concerto blares out. Shortly* GLORIA *turns on light, shuts phonograph.* BEN *is not seen.* GLORIA *puts on her skirt, her shoes.* BEN *enters from the kitchen. They are both vaguely uncomfortable*)

GLORIA
Will I be seeing you again?

BEN
It's up to you.

GLORIA
I'd like to, very much. I wasn't lying about anything I said.
    (*Putting on makeup*)
You are going to try, aren't you?

BEN
Maybe. It's something I always wanted.

THE TIGER

GLORIA

Then you'll certainly get it. I know you will. Look. I can come every Thursday night and help you with your French. We can study together. You won't have any trouble passing the exam this time.
   (*Picking up book*)
Here's what I'd like you to do by next week. Read from the beginning to . . . here. And do these exercises on pages five and six. Is that too much for you?

BEN

I can do it. What about your husband?

GLORIA
   (*Seated on arm of upholstered chair*)
He wouldn't know if the roof fell on him. He'll think I'm playing bridge with the girls. We can meet at the same place.

BEN

In front of the stationery store?

GLORIA

Seven-thirty.

BEN

Seven-thirty.

GLORIA

Do I get a good-night kiss?
   (*He bends over, kisses her*)

THE TIGER

That wasn't good enough.
>(*He kisses her again*)

That was a little better.
>(*He kisses her a third time*)

That . . . That was a lot better. Next time I come I'm going to give this place a good cleaning. It's a mess.
>(*At top of steps*)

Bon soir, my darling.

BEN

Bon soir.
>(GLORIA *exits.* BEN *sits in upholstered chair and studies his lesson in the French book as the light fades*)